Soon You Will Understand…
The Meaning of Life

Soon You Will Understand...
The Meaning of Life

William Blank

Writers Club Press

New York Lincoln Shanghai

Soon You Will Understand...The Meaning of Life

Writers Club Press
an imprint of iUniverse, Inc.

For information address:
iUniverse
2021 Pine Lake Road, Suite 100
Lincoln, NE 68512
www.iuniverse.com

ISBN: 0-595-26044-6 (Pbk)
ISBN: 0-595-65507-6 (Cloth)

Printed in the United States of America

Table of Contents

Introduction

The Talmud teaches:

Just before a baby is born,

>an angel shows it everything there is to know

>and learn

>on Earth.

Then at the moment of birth,

>the angel touches the infant's upper lip,

>and the child forgets everything.

We spend the rest of our lives

>remembering

>what the angel showed us.

1

This is a generic guide

    to the meaning of life.

It does not describe one view

    of the meaning of life

    and recommend you adopt it.

It helps you remember

    what the angel showed you.

The angel showed you

    the meaning of life.

In case you have not remembered yet,

    here is what the angel showed you.

1. You Will…

Land Here

Just exactly as if you are landing a spaceship

    from another galaxy,

    your soul enters your body

    and lands here on Earth.

Perhaps you come from out of nowhere,

    out of nothingness.

Or else you had a previous existence somewhere,

    in another realm

    or in this realm,

    and you have forgotten it.

Perhaps you land here

    of your own free choice.

Or some cosmic force

    some karma

    beyond you

    causes you to land on this planet;

    and you have no choice.

No matter.

This is Earth.

You land

    and stay for a while.

2. You Will…

Have Tasks

You come here to do certain

specific

things.

You may have one task

or many.

Your tasks may be obvious to you.

or you may need time,

effort,

maybe struggle

even to clarify

your tasks.

You may never quite even clarify your task

until the moment

your time in this body

ends.

You may work on your task for years

before you realize,

"This is my task."

The tasks you came to perform

may take the whole of your life

or be done in an instant.

You may be aware

you are performing your life task

while you do it.

You may perform your task quickly,

hardly noticing

anything special,

unaware

you are doing the task

you came to do

while you do it.

Your task may be so easy,

obvious and

natural,

you never even wonder,

"What is my task?"

Your unique blend

of talents and interests

may lead you

to your task,

and you just do it.

Or, your task may be a constant,

unpleasant

struggle

you fight

every step of the way.

Your task may be noble and wonderful

    and gain you

    recognition,

    rewards

    and honors.

Or, it may be simple,

    totally unnoticeable

    by anyone else.

3. You Will…

Work to Survive

You will be born

    with a powerful

    innate desire

    to remain alive.

You will do almost anything

    to continue living.

At some point

    you may discover

    some limits,

and allow your life

to end.

4. You Will…

Have Experiences

Every thought you have,

Every action you take,

Every feeling you perceive

> *is an experience.*

Experiences are neither good nor evil.

Some experiences are short,

> *some are long.*

Some experiences will be fun,

> *others will be excruciating.*

Sometimes experiences seem interconnected,

sometimes they seem random.

They are simply experiences.

5. You Will...

Have a Body, Emotions, Thoughts and a Soul

Your experiences will come to you through four modalities:

> *physical,*

> *emotional,*

> *mental*

> *and spiritual.*

Your body will give you physical messages of

> *sensation,*

> *movement,*

pain and

pleasure.

Your emotional mechanism's feelings

will attract you

and repel you

in different directions,

sometimes conflicting.

Your mind's thoughts

will make logical inferences

and judgments

about your experience.

Your soul's intuitions

will guide you

to realize

the deepest subtleties

of your experience

and its meaning.

6. You Will…

Have Challenges

Some of your experiences will be difficult.

They will bring you pain and suffering.

You may wish with all your heart

   that some experience

   did not come your way.

You may find joy in the challenge

   of an experience,

   even when the pain

   is most severe.

Each difficult experience

is a challenge,

an opportunity

to continue.

7. You Will…

Decide

You will have the experience

of choosing

or selecting.

More than one viable option

will lie before you.

You will experience weighing

the advantages

and disadvantages

of each,

as best you can.

You will perceive yourself

    picking one

    and letting go of the other.

Some experiences of deciding

    will be very difficult;

    others

    scarcely worth noting.

Your decisions will have consequences.

The consequences of a choice

    may be significant

    or trivial.

The ultimate consequences of a choice

    may be very different

    from their first appearance.

8. You Will…

Grow

You will experience a process of

change

in yourself.

One moment you may be paralyzed with fear

of what lies ahead;

the next moment you will feel

confident and knowledgeable

having walked through the fear.

The change may come gradually

with no clear moment

or division.

Whether the outcome you receive is

what you were hoping for

or very different,

you will grow

through each experience.

9. You Will…

Mature

You will experience stages in your life.

You begin as a single cell

    and grow

    until you are born

    as a small infant.

You continue to grow

    through the lifecycle

    for as long as you survive:

    childhood,

    adolescence,

young adulthood,

adulthood,

maturity,

supermaturity,

elderhood,

and frailty.

You may not live through all of the available stages.

Each segment contains

> *physical, emotional, mental and spiritual*

> *growth experiences*

> *unique to itself.*

Stages may end and begin

> *suddenly,*

> *or segué into one another*

> *gradually.*

As you conclude a stage you may feel relief

> *or remorse*

> *that it is over.*

Once you move through a stage,

it is over;

you cannot go back.

10. You Will…

Have Guides

You will receive assistance

through this process.

You will find various teachers and mentors

who will share their experiences

and help you read the signposts

along your way.

You will have birth parents

who will be your central guides;

or you will find surrogates for them.

If you do not find

another person

to be your guide,

you may find you can look deep within

to find guidance.

11. You Will...

Communicate

You will find diverse modes

through which to exchange information

with other beings.

You will learn

spoken and

written languages.

You will find ways to communicate

with your body.

You will communicate

   many things

   through your actions.

You will discover a variety of

   visual,

   auditory

   and tactile arts

   through which to express

   your thoughts

   and feelings.

You may also discern very subtle,

   almost unnamable

   communications

   which can be the most powerful.

12. You Will…

Gain Skills

Every experience requires abilities.

You will master

> *diverse skills*

> *for an endless array*

> *of available activities.*

You will have innate talents for some skills;

> *they will come to you so easily*

> *they seem automatic.*

Others will require many hours

    or even years to master;

    even after much practice,

    you may never

    become proficient at them.

13. You Will…

Play

You will participate in games

at every stage of life.

You will play with others

or by yourself

in a variety of contests.

Some games will be fun;

some will be deadly serious.

Some games will be highly competitive;

others will be totally noncompetitive.

You may compete individually .

    or as a team,

    against others

    or only against yourself.

Some games will offer

    physical or

    material rewards

    or acclaim from others

    if you are successful at them.

14. You Will…

Learn How Things Work

You will study diverse subjects,

   each of which attempts to explain

   some details

   of how the world works.

You may study them in a school

   or by your own investigation.

You will acquire minimal knowledge of some,

   and you will dive deeply in others.

You will learn aspects of mathematics,

geography,

physics,

sociology,

economics,

biology,

astronomy,

anthropology,

history,

engineering,

the arts,

chemistry,

philosophy

and religion.

15. You Will…

Do Work

You will be inclined to produce something

or to provide a service

for which you receive compensation.

Your work will earn you the food and shelter

you need to survive

and less essential things

for your enjoyment.

You may work many long hours each day

or a much smaller time segment.

Your work may be an important

    component

    of your life task.

Or, your work may ensure your physical survival

    or comfort,

    allowing you to fulfill the tasks

    you came here to do.

16. You Will…

Belong to a Tribe

You will find a group of individuals

   to which you feel connected,

   either by birth

   or by affinity.

You will experience a bond

   with the other members

   of this tribe

   or with the tribal entity itself.

You will be subject to the rules your tribe makes.

You will have a position within the tribe

   based on your birth

   or your talents.

Your position will affect your activities

   within the tribe

   and throughout your life.

You may find you are a part of more than one tribe

   or that your tribe is part

   of a tribal confederation.

17. You Will…

Have God(s)

You will find deities

    to which to attach

    your greatest fears

    and devotions.

You may have one god or many.

You may learn about your god or gods

    from others,

    or you may experience them

    yourself.

Your gods may be attached specifically to your tribe

   or they may claim a wider domain.

Your gods may be projections

   of human experience

   or they may be something beyond

   human experience

   with a reality

   all their own.

18. You Will…

Celebrate

At certain special moments of your life

You will mark transitions:

you will sing,

you will dance,

you will talk to your gods,

you will do special rituals

to celebrate.

You may celebrate alone

or in a group.

You will celebrate those moments when you

or someone in your tribe

passes

from one stage of the growth process

to another.

Special good times

and special bad times

call for celebrations.

Repeating seasons of each year

ask for celebrations as well.

19. You Will…

Find Friends

You will be drawn to certain individuals

with whom you will share

some of your experiences

more closely.

You will experience strong connections

with some of the friends

you find.

Some will remain friends

for a short time,

while others may remain

close to you

for long periods.

20. You Will…

Find Mates

You will be drawn to bond strongly

with a partner.

Like friends, mates may remain

for short or long periods of time.

Your mate may be your closest,

special friend

or a friend with whom you share

a set of experiences.

You may have one mate

for your lifetime

or a series of mates

at different times.

21. You Will…

Acquire Wealth

You will earn rewards for your work

or in payment for your other activities.

Some wealth will have material value

which you can exchange

for physical objects

or services

you desire

or which your tribe convinces you

you desire.

Other types of wealth are more subtle

and not exchangeable.

You will decide which types of wealth

you will pursue

and how vigorously

to pursue

each of them.

22. You Will…

Amass Power

You will exert control

    through your physical being,

    your wealth,

    your office,

    your abilities,

    your personal energy

    or your facility for managing other people.

With this power you will make some things happen

    the way you want them

    to happen.

If your power is great enough,

others will do

what you would like them to do,

even if it is not in their own best interest.

23. You Will…

Feel Sensuality

You will experience delights of the senses.

Food,

touch,

music,

aroma,

nature,

movement,

art

and dance

will intensify your enjoyment

of your time here.

24. You Will…

Experience Sex

You will feel an intense yearning

of your body

to touch another person

most deeply.

The intensity of that touch

may take the experience

beyond the body,

to bond closely with the other person

or to procreate,

to make the lifecycle begin anew.

25. You Will…

Create a Home

You will experience the urge

to create your own space

where you spend most of your time,

where you belong,

where you experience roots.

It may be in the place of your origin

or you may feel compelled to travel

elsewhere

to create it.

You may wish to share your home

with those closest to you.

26. You Will…

Express Artistic

You will express yourself

or create something

existing independently

of yourself.

What you form may last

for generations

or for only a moment.

The content of your expression

may take physical form

or it may reach out

through other media.

27. You Will…

Display

You will feel the urge

to show others

whatever you have earned,

whatever you have created,

whatever you have learned,

whatever you have become.

You may wish to display it

publicly,

to have others to view it.

Or, you may display it

privately

just for yourself

or a few others.

28. You Will…

Accumulate Wisdom

As your experiences broaden,

you will become familiar

with experience itself.

You will recognize its ebb and flow,

And you will become more comfortable

with its changes.

You may experience the desire to share

this wisdom

you accumulate

with others.

29. You Will…

Break Rules

You will do things your tribe decided

    was forbidden

    or others told you

    is wrong.

You may do some things

    that something within

    you

    says

    you should not do.

You will test some of the limits

    by lying,

    cheating,

    stealing,

    or doing other things

    that may cause pain.

You may get caught by

    those in power

    and you may have to pay

    a penalty.

30. You Will…

Parent

You will participate in the birth process

and the child rearing process.

You may give birth to a child.

You may take a central role

in guiding a child

through life's stages.

You may experience parenting

as bringing whatever you create

into existence.

31. You Will…

Teach

You will feel impelled to share

some of what you learn

through life's experience

with others.

You may teach

in a classroom

or through any mode of communications

available to you.

32. You Will…

Expel Waste

You will experience the need to let go

   of some things.

You will discharge waste

   from your body,

   from your physical surroundings,

   from your emotional apparatus,

   from your mind

   and from your spirit.

You will seek ways to discharge your wastes

   in a manner that is safe

   for yourself

   and your environment.

33. You Will…

Heal

You will experience disease,

pain

or sickness in yourself,

in those around you

or even in the whole planet.

You will feel the urge to find remedies

and treatments,

emotional support,

and focused energy

to aid in the healing process.

34. You Will…

Fail

In some activities, you will not reach the goal

you desired.

You will feel pain at your failure.

At times, the pain of failure

will become very severe.

35. You Will…

Lose

Everything you have is impermanent.

Things you work for

    and you value

    will not remain with you

    forever.

People close to you

    will die.

You will feel pain

    with loss.

36. You Will…

Cry

At times your emotional mode will become extremely

highly charged.

You will be moved to cry,

either in pain

or in joy or

in some mixture of both.

37. You Will...

Love

You will experience the urge to connect

intensely

in physical,

emotional,

mental

and spiritual modes.

Your love toward

other beings,

nature,

gods

or life itself

will draw you very close

to the other,

to identify with it

most intimately

or to lose yourself in it.

38. You Will…

Accept Others

You will become comfortable with the diversity

among other beings.

You will experience accepting

other beings

exactly as they are,

in their own unique perfection,

exactly as you would like them

to accept you

as you are.

39. You Will…

Change States of Consciousness

You will go through fundamental alterations

in the quality of your experience.

Either spontaneously

or as a result of prayer,

meditation,

ritual,

song

or special foods.

You will experience

    great love,

    wisdom,

    serenity,

    or connection

    to a god

    or nature.

Experiencing altered states of consciousness

    will affect

    all of your other experiences.

You will experience yourself

    transformed

    into a different being.

40. You Will…

Open to New Depths

The limits of your experience

will expand

to include intuition

or a transcending of this realm

or a oneness

with something much greater

than yourself.

You may experience yourself leaving your body

or knowing things before they occur.

You may experience powerful synchronicity.

You may lose your sense of yourself

   as an independent being

And experience yourself as one

   with the infinite wholeness

   of the universe.

41. You Will…

Write Your Story

You will experience the urge to pass on

the tale

of your lifetime.

You may tell your story

to those most likely

to remember it;

Or, you may transmit it

in some other

artistic form.

42. You Will…

Die

You will leave your body.

Everyone else will experience your body

becoming lifeless

and begin to decay.

You will no longer be present

in this plane

in your physical form,

But some aspects

of your emotional,

mental and

spiritual modes

may continue

to be experienced by others.

43. You Will…

Enter a Next Realm

Your emotional, mental or spiritual modes

will enter some sort of afterlife.

You may be aware

of your continuity

between this lifetime

and the next realm

or you may not.

You may experience reincarnation

> *into the body of another being*

> *and begin another lifetime.*

The nature of your next realm may be determined

> *by your activities*

> *and experiences in this lifetime.*

The nature of the next realm may be extremely

> *subtle*

> *and indescribable.*

44. You Will…

Be Remembered

Those who knew you will recall

who you were,

what you did,

what you gave

and the qualities you manifested.

If you physically parented another,

your genetic material will continue

within them as well.

Others' remembering you

    will continue to affect them

    directly

    and the whole planet

    indirectly

    in subtle

    and not so subtle ways.

Who Wrote This?

The author of Soon You Will Understand...The Meaning of Life is a middle-aged guy named Bill who has walked through a big part of the extreme yin and yang of human possibilities.

His life experiences include:

- *Ordination in a mainstream spiritual tradition*

- *Serving a number of years as a clergyperson in that tradition*

- *Writing a well-received book*

- *Running several marathons and triathlons*

- *Earned some advanced degrees*

- *Married over 30 years*

- *Sired and is raising three daughters*

- *Spending a lot of time hanging out in a variety of diverse spiritual environments*

- *Being a professional fundraiser for a nonprofit organization*

- *Practicing hypnotherapy for smoking cessation and past life regression*

Currently earning his living as a writer of user guides for software products, websites and related communications in the information technology industry

All of the material in "Soon You Will Understand...The Meaning of Life" came to him in a sudden flash of insight.

Contact Author

To contact the author, email:

bill@themeaningoflife.org

What Do the Graphics Mean?

They mean

whatever you want them to mean.

0-595-26044-6